Small
Packages

WORSHIP STORIES FOR CHILDREN

ERNST H. NUSSMANN

C.S.S. Publishing Co., Inc.

Lima, Ohio

SMALL PACKAGES

Copyright © 1988 by
The C.S.S. Publishing Company, Inc.
Lima, Ohio

Library of Congress Cataloging-in-Publication Data

Nussman, Ernst H., 1912-1987
   Small packages: worship stories for children/Ernst H. Nussman.
      p. cm.
   Includes indexes.
   ISBN 1-556-73027-6
   1. Children's sermons. I. Title.
BV4315.N87   1988
252'.53—dc19   87-31682

8812 / ISBN 1-55673-027-6

Table of Contents

Just To Be With Him	Psalm 73:28	*9*
Use, *What You Have*	Matthew 25:25	*10*
Spend It For The Best	Deuteronomy 30:19	*12*
A Pot Of Glue	1 Thessalonians 1:3	*13*
Mirrors	Psalm 51:10	*15*
Table Prayer	Ephesians 5:20	*17*
Targets	1 Corinthians 14:12	*19*
A Pretzel And A Prayer	Luke 11:1	*21*
In My Mind	John 13:17	*23*
Just Where Is God?	Psalm 139:1-10	*25*
Somebody Is Following You	1 Timothy 4:12	*27*
Popularity Winner	Romans 12:10	*29*
Blame	Luke 15:18	*31*
The Three Sons	Matthew 5:47	*33*
Birthdays	Psalm 33:12	*35*
What Would The Whole World Be Worth . . .	John 13:35	*36*
Trap — Beware	Proverbs 15:5	*38*
Be The Best	Philippians 3:14	*40*
Weeding	1 Samuel 12:24	*41*
Special Glasses	Jeremiah 5:21	*42*
The Huddle	Matthew 18:20	*44*
Snap Judgment	Romans 14:13	*45*
Light Of The World	John 1:5	*46*
A Penny	Matthew 6:33	*48*
Silent Whistle — Silent Speech	1 Samuel 3:9	*50*
Like A Hole In Your Sock	2 Corinthians 2:7	*51*
Simple Simon	Matthew 13:46	*52*
A Weight Can Be A "Lift"	Matthew 11:30	*54*
Fall Forward	Revelations 2:10	*56*
Buckets	Matthew 13:23	*57*
Thread	Proverbs 20:11	*59*

Taming The "Wild"	Isaiah 50:4	60
A Proud And Happy Feeling	Matthew 6:4	62
Don't Point	Luke 6:41	64
Just Checking Up	Psalm 39:23	65
Weaknesses	Song of Solomon 2:15	66
Being Brave	Deuteronomy 31:6	67
Sticks	Ephesians 4:13	69
How Are Your Ears?	Exodus 20:19	71
Medicine	Romans 15:4	73
Tool-Box Or Trash-Can?	Deuteronomy 4:9	75
Looks	1 Peter 3:3	76
Spring	Proverbs 4:23	78
Repetition	Ezra 9:6	80
Magic Carpets	2 Corinthians 8:30	81
Yardsticks	Deuteronomy 10:12	83
A Boat	2 Timothy 1:12	85
Right For The Job	Matthew 10:31	87
Anonymous!	Matthew 10:42	88
From The Inside Out	Luke 6:45	90
Processional Caterpillars	Psalm 27:11	92
God's Hands	Psalm 143:10	94
Does It Show?	Matthew 5:16	95
Impressions	Psalm 85:8	96
Getting Results	1 Corinthians 12:4	98
Cheerful Givers	Luke 2:4	99
Failures	1 John 1:9	101
Heaven's Gates	Mark 9:35	102
Joined Together	Psalm 133:1	104
Topical Index		106
Scriptural Index		108

Acknowledgments

New ideas, like babies, are conceived through a mysterious alchemy; and though these blendings of old ideas may sparkle with their own uniqueness, they will always carry the marks of their "roots."

Many of the ideas to be found in this book are obviously not original . . . some have their roots in

another's anecdote,
   a fable,
      the morning's news,
         a shared experience,
            a memory, and of course —
               an oft-told Bible story.

But they all have taken on an essence which makes them my own. I really do not know the true "sources" of the root ideas, but I am grateful for them, and only hope that they might inspire and help to shape yours as you read and use these children's sermons.

These pages include enough detail to be considered "complete" — and yet are presented in "outline" form in order to encourage you, the user, to extend the stories in a way that will fit your particular audience, and to fill in the "gaps" with a rich imagination. "Props" are often helpful and are sometimes indicated. Let your listeners be *participants* as often as possible — so that the "ideas" may actually come to be their own!

— Ernst H. Nussmann

Introduction

A children's sermon is a way of exposing young listeners to the *Truths* about life — not only to the engaging physical truths, but to the compelling and deeply spiritual truths, as well. Children of *all* ages are ready and even eager to accept and incorporate religious values into the blue-prints which they are already drawing for their lives. In response to appropriately prepared material, they have a remarkable capacity to absorb a profound message; and where they may be unable to digest the whole meaning, they do at least get a "feeling" for major themes and ideas.

For these reasons, the children's sermon has become an accepted feature in many contemporary worship services; however, for many leaders who may not have a natural talent for communicating with children, or who are without any special training in this area, it presents a special challenge. This collection of children's sermons is intended to assist both professional and lay religious leaders, as well as parents — and to provide examples for the kinds of children's sermons which they can then create for themselves.

There are several principles which have guided the development of this collection of children's sermons, and which may be useful for those who will adapt and use these lessons:

Children's sermons are for "rubbing shoulders with the truth" and cannot afford to be of the flimsy, unrealistic material of which Santa Claus or the Easter Bunny are made — and which sooner or later will have to be rejected or reconstructed for the *real* world.

Children's sermons provide "food for thought," but ought not be pre-digested "namby-pamby" platitudes. They can be prepared both in a way that makes them acceptable and easily absorbed — and in a way that enables the children to have a share in finding the truth which they contain.

Children's sermons are *worship, not an "intrusion" into the worship service*! Their themes can be in harmony with that of the hymns, Scriptures, prayers, and the "regular" sermon of the hour. Rather than an intrusion upon the mood of worship, the children's sermon should flow with that mood. Hence, it is *not* at all necessary that children of given ages sit on the chancel steps or at the pastor's knees — busily watching the folks in the congregation, as well as being watched by them. How much better for children — of *all* ages — to listen unself-consciously, seated with parents or brothers, sisters, friends, and others in the congregational family, as part of the whole gathering, listening to a message of value and use for *everyone* present — including adults! In fact, integrating the children's sermon into the rest of the service serves to reinforce for children that they do not need to "tune out" the "other" or "adult" part of the service, but that at some level there is something for them to enjoy or learn from each of the various forms of worship.

Children's sermons need never be presented as something which, like "babytalk," adults consider without worth or beneath their dignity. Adults can find themselves just as absorbed by the children's sermons as the children, and gladly confess, "that children's sermon this morning did more for me today than the 'regular' one!"

Children's sermons are most effective when they are alive — that is, when they are *told* (or even dramatized by some of the children themselves) instead of being read. The sermons in this collection are therefore presented in a suggestive rather than literal form — an invitation for users to "edit" them, to expand or change the material, to meet the need at hand.

Children's sermons are aimed sometimes at the very young, other times at early teens or youth, often at the children in between — and even now and then at the adults. Each person, at whatever age, gleans from the simple and direct, sometimes humorous or dramatic message, that which he or she wishes — or is able — to accept as part of his or her value system and life!

Lay leaders — and parents — will find these children's sermons as useable and valuable as will the pastor or professional storyteller. They provide a pattern for learning to use our experiences, and the things we all hear and see around us, as a basis for understanding our world and for developing mature spiritual values.

Dedication

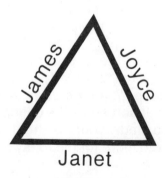

Janet

Just To Be With Him

Do you really understand why it is that you, and your family, and so many friends, and lots of strangers come to Church . . . and worship — Sunday after Sunday — and go away feeling fresh, confident, strong, and "good"?

Maybe a story will help to explain it.

This is a story about a busy doctor working away at his desk in the den at home, when his little boy sidled into the room, and stood silently at his father's side.

The father noticed, but, preoccupied with his work, absently slipped his hand into his pocket, drew out a coin, and offered it to the boy.

"I don't want any money, Daddy," said the boy, simply.

Still engrossed in his work, the father went on writing . . . but, opening the desk drawer, pulled out a couple pieces of candy and passed them to his son.

"I don't want any candy, Daddy," assured the boy.

At which the father put his work aside . . . "What *do* you want then?"

"I only wanted to be with you!" replied the boy with a voice full of love.

Mostly we come to Church —
not to get something special,
or to ask a big favor . . .
but *just to be with Him*!
    That makes a big difference
            in the way we think,
            in the way we feel,
            in the way we look — and act!

Use, What You Have!

I saw a man whittling a little match —
   with a great big machete (the kind of knife men
   use to cut their ways through the jungle). It
   seemed so silly — I thought I must be dreaming!

But then I saw a man using a steam shovel —
   to transplant pansies in his garden;
I saw a woman using a bulldozer —
   to clean the crumbs off her kitchen linoleum;
I saw a bunch of fellows on a snack break, using a
   pile-driver — to crack peanuts;
I saw a teenager using a huge derrick —
   for hanging his clothes in the closet.

By this time, I *knew* I was dreaming.
   It would be foolish to use such giant, wonderful
      tools to do such little jobs!
   Those tools weren't doing even a small part of
      what they were made to do.

Oh, I just had to be dreaming!

But, I've seen things just as foolish when I *wasn't*
   dreaming!

   Boys and girls using a great talent for reading —
      only for comics;
   using a great talent for speech —
      only for wisecracks;
   using a great talent for thinking —
      only for "getting by";

using a great talent for helping others —
only for entertaining themselves.

God has given each of us some bulldozer-sized tools,
talents, and skills — in our brains, eyes, voices, hands!
I hope you're not just wasting yours on "piddling" sized
jobs. Ask Him to show you what to *do* with them!

Spend It For The Best

Yesterday I was in a store, waiting to pay for my purchase at the cash register . . . which was close to the candy counter.

There — looking hard and carefully at every one of the different kinds of candy — was a little boy, about as big as you! In his hand was a quarter.

His Dad was kind of gruff — like Dad's are sometimes — in a hurry, I guess, and probably embarrassed, because the candy clerk was getting impatient. "Hurry up!" he said. "Come on! You can't take all day. All you've got is one quarter — just take anything!"

The little boy didn't say a word, but went right on looking, as if to say, "That's just it . . . I only have one quarter, so I've got to spend it carefully!"

And do you know, he finally left without spending it! I'm sure he thought, "I'll wait 'till next time!" He was determined to be sure he spent that quarter for the *best* . . . something he *really wanted*!

You'd be careful, too, if you only had one quarter to spend. You have more quarters, of course . . . but you only have *one life* to spend!

How are you spending it?
surely not in bed — sleeping;
or in front of the TV — hardly thinking or moving;
or making "mud pies."

There are as many ways for you to spend your life as there are "kinds of candy," I guess. You can't choose them all . . .

but you *can* choose to *Spend Your Life* for the *Best*!

A Pot Of Glue

A man who had been a member of a big church in the east died, and — since he had been a rather outstanding fellow — the question came up: what should be done in his memory?

It was pretty easy to decide on a stained glass window for the sanctuary . . . but with what picture or symbol? Well, the committee discussed possibilities:

It could be an angel (but it would have to be a tall, strong one — *not* a cute little one with a halo and feathery wings);
It could be an anchor (his faith was like that);
It could be a Bible (he read it often and loved it);
It could be a harp (he really did enjoy singing).

Then one man said, "I would like to see it be . . . a *pot of glue*!" "You must be kidding!" exclaimed the others, as their eyes popped and their mouths dropped open. "No," came the suggestion again, "for this is exactly what our friend was — a pot of strong glue! He did so much to hold things together. A lot of things would have gone to pieces around here if it had not been for him!"

The others agreed . . . he had stuck to his faith in such a way that he had influenced others to stick too — and, as a result, they had *stuck together*! And so it happened that among the other windows showing the Cross, wheat, grapes, and the Triangle of the Trinity, there is one which shows . . . a pot of glue!

That's a good Christian symbol, isn't it? The world

needs people who will stick to what is right, and stick to each other . . . people who have the "stuff" to hold things together — at home, at church, in the community, and the world!

Will *you* be one? Maybe folks will never place a window for you — but I hope everyone will feel that you deserve one!

Please pass the glue!

Mirrors

When Lady Mary Montague (who lived in the 1700s) died, she had not used a mirror for eleven years! That was because she did not like what she saw there! After eleven years without a mirror . . . do you suppose the people who lived around her liked what they saw? How would you look, without a mirror, for just one week . . . or even one day?

> I know — each hair would be sticking out in
> a different direction;
> — here and there your face would be
> egg-yellow, chocolate-brown,
> kool-aid pink, dirt-black,
> — and you'd go around not knowing
> whether you wore a pleasant or
> grouchy expression.

A mirror shows you what you *look* like — on the *outside*! It's good to "check up" with one now and then — so you can improve your looks.

Coming here for Sunday church school and worship is a lot like looking into a mirror — only here you see what you *are* like on the *inside*!

> You notice spots and streaks of selfishness,
> unkindness, carelessness, weakness, and say:
> "Am I like that? I'll have to do something
> about it."

> Now and then you notice something about
> yourself
> that you like and which makes you glad, and
> leads you to say: "I'll work for more of
> that."

16

People are foolish to try to get along without a mirror — it helps so much to improve how they *look* on the *outside*.

People are foolish to try to get along without Sunday church school and the church — it could help a whole lot to improve what they *are* on the *inside*.

See you in Church — regularly!

Table Prayer

Once, when a Sunday church school teacher asked her students whether they prayed before meals at home, one boy answered,

"Oh, we don't have to . . . my mom's a good cook!"

He certainly had the wrong idea about the reasons for mealtime prayer, didn't he! As though you prayed because you needed God's help and protection — in case anything was wrong with the food.

Why *do* you pray before meals? (Maybe it's been a long time since you've given it any thought . . . or have prayed.)

Well, for one thing, you show that you realize all good things come from God. (Though Mom & Dad work at it, they couldn't provide anything without God.)

For another, it is a good way of saying "Thank You" for the gifts we really haven't earned . . . and don't really deserve.

For a third thing, it makes us remember that God is near, *even* when we aren't thinking about it.

But, best of all, it is like an invitation to God to be our guest —

not over in some corner of the room, but as a part of the family circle,

influencing the conversation,

making different the spirit of the home,

"feeding" us the things that will make us grow — not only as strong bodies, but as fine persons!

You might want to use this prayer at your table today:

I fold my hands and bow my head,
  To thank You for my daily bread! Amen

You may want to make up your own prayer, too!

Targets

An F.B.I. agent was visiting a community in the mountains. Everywhere he went he saw targets, "bull's-eyes" (like this one), on the sides of sheds, the ends of boxes, on tree trunks. The place was full of them. And *every* target had a bullet hole exactly in the center! He was amazed, and said he'd like to meet the marksman who had such perfect aim and skill.

When he finally located him, the agent asked with a kind of awe in his voice, "How in the world do you do it?"

"Easy," the man grinned. "I shoot first — and then paint a target around the hole!"

I wouldn't give a dime for his "aim" or "skill." But then, I wouldn't give a dime for some of *yours* either!

You shoot wherever you please (do as you like,
    the easy thing, whatever you happen to want),
then "paint the target" with excuses and arguments
    to make whatever you've done look good and
    right!
I'll never think much of you . . .
and you'll never think much of yourself . . .
till you make targets — like the ones Jesus already
    set up:
      "KIND"   "THOUGHTFUL"   "PURE"
   "LOVING"   "HONEST"   "HELPFUL"
          "DECENT" . . .

Start aiming at them, and then work hard at perfecting your skill so as to be able to hit closer and closer — always closer to the *center*!

(Use a cardboard with a bull's-eye drawn on it and a hole in the center as an introduction. If possible, use similar targets for use in closing, with the words "KIND," "THOUGHTFUL," etc ... perhaps with some holes not so close to the center.)

A Pretzel And A Prayer

I'm sure you know what this is. Of course, a *pretzel*!
And what do you think of when you see one?
   I know — beer! "Beer and pretzels have always gone
   together," people say. But this is not so!
When pretzels were first made they were made to
remind people of something quite different from beer.
Believe it or not, pretzels were originated around A.D.
600 by a devout monk in Southern France who wanted
to use up the scraps of dough left over after he had
finished making the bread and rolls in the monastery
bakery.
   At first, he just baked those scraps in whatever odd
shapes they happened to be in, and gave them to the
hungry boys and girls always hanging around.
   Then he got the idea that he could teach those boys
and girls something good at the same time he fed them.
So, he formed the dough in the shape we now know as
the pretzel — to represent the children's little arms
folded in prayer. (*Demonstrate*) Then he began to give
them to the children as a reward for learning their
prayers.
   And so pretzels came to be a reminder to *everybody*
of the sacred privilege of prayer. It didn't have to be a
cathedral,
   a bell,
      or a book . . . just a simple piece of dough could
remind people that when they hold up hands (*demon-strate*) in humility and sincerity,
   God hears — and we are blessed — anywhere,
   anytime!
From now on, when I see a pretzel, I'm going to

forget about beer, and think of a child's arms crossed in prayer,

    and of the love of God and trust in God that are at the heart of a child's faith when he or she prays!

In My Mind

A certain man who was driving down the road *intended* to
> put on the brakes,
>> slow down, and then
>>> stop at a railroad crossing . . .

but, there was a terrible smash-up, and he lost his life!

Why? Because he didn't *really*
>> put on the brakes,

slow down, and then stop at that railroad crossing —
he only *intended* to!

If "intending" took the place of "doing":

you'd know a lot — for you certainly intend to study;

you'd always be on the honor roll — for you certainly intend to get A's;

you'd be looked up to as the most worthwhile kid on your block — for you certainly intend to amount to something;

you'd be picked for "first team" in athletics —
for you certainly intend to play without error.

But, there's a long way between "intending" and "producing."

How often we are like some water-fountains, gleaming white, shiny silver — the complete set-up — with every intention of giving folks a drink, but never quite coming across with the water!

How sad it is, when we are a disappointment to others — and to ourselves. Our "intentions" are so good! Well, what shall we do? *Intend* a little harder? No. Intentions aren't enough. Paul found that out. He says, "The good things I intend to do — I don't. And the bad things I intend not to do — I do. Intentions left me hanging in mid-air until I let God take over and rule my life. Now I can do all things as I really *intend*."

With God's help, you and I can carry out our intentions to be Christian, and to *act* like Christians!

Just Where *Is* God?

An atheist once painted a big sign on a board fence, for everybody to see:

GOD IS NOWHERE!

A kid on his way home from Sunday church school read what the atheist had written:

GOD IS NOW HERE!

The kid made a mistake, didn't he? ... Or was it the atheist who made the mistake — and the kid who was right!

God *is now here* — and is always so!

A little fish overheard some older fish talking about the ocean. It sounded like something wonderful, so, thinking he'd like to see it, he set out in search of the sea. Along the way he met several other young fish. Of each he asked, "Hey, where's the ocean? I'd like to find it."

The first answered, "I don't know — I'm too little to know."

The second said, "I don't know — I'm too busy to find out."

The third shouted over his shoulder, "I don't know — and what's more, I don't care!"

Finally, he asked an old fish, who smiled and said, "Why, little fish, you are right in it!"

It is everywhere around you!
you have been surrounded by it all your life!

You wonder where God is? — and would like to find him?

Well, He is a Spirit and invisible, but he is
all around you and within you;
He has surrounded you with his presence
all your life;
He is closer than breathing, and nearer
than hands and feet;
He knows you and loves you and is ready
to help you!

You don't have to go far away to find him. You will discover him as soon as you get over thinking you are "too little,"
"too busy,"
or you "don't care"!

(Begin with large lettering like painting on a fence:
G O D I S N O W H E R E !)

Somebody Is Following You

Don't look now, but somebody is following *you*!
Maybe you didn't know that? You think *you* are doing
all the following . . .
in the footsteps of your teachers,
your parents,
the big kids on the street,
great people you know about,
so that you can get to be like them?

Well, somebody is following YOU . . . to be like YOU!
(It is usually somebody smaller and younger.)
YOU stick your tongue out at your playmates:
he watches — and does it too!
YOU cheat at a game:
he watches — and does it too!
YOU draw pictures and whisper during the worship
at church:
he watches — and does it too!
Of course, when
YOU are gracious and courteous to your playmates:
he watches — and does that too!, when
YOU are honest, even when it causes you to lose:
he watches — and does that too!, when
YOU are reverent and thoughtful in church:
he watches — and does that too!

So, you see, where you are going and what you do
is more important than you thought . . .
not only because *you* will finally "get there" and
"be like that," but
because Somebody Else is *following you there*, and
is *going to be like that too*!

When you choose — what to do, and what kind of person to be,

you are choosing for yourself
— and for that somebody following you!

Popularity Winner

I know a family of boys and girls in which, if a vote were taken as to which member of the family was the "most popular," the result might be *surprising*!

I believe the children would all agree it was the "newest" member —

the small,
> wiggly,
>> playful,
>>> brown,
>>>> fluffy-haired . . . *dog*!

I'll tell you some reasons why:

He never comes "grumpy" to breakfast — as though he had gotten out of bed on the wrong side.

Whether it is cloudy or bright outside, it's always a "good morning" for the pup.

He never says he'll not play unless everything goes his way.

He never sulks and is always ready to join in whatever is going on.

He makes the best of everything.

He never lets yesterday's disappointments — or tomorrow's worries — spoil today's chances for happiness!

He doesn't sit around and pout, because somebody left him out in the rain yesterday or because he is tired of his food.

He doesn't whine and fret or worry, because tomorrow the kids will be back at school and leave him all alone, or because some bigger dog may take his bone.

These are some pretty good suggestions from a dog! Try them — you might go up a big notch in *your* family's rating — not only as "most popular,"
but as the happiest, too!

Blame

Mother was working in the kitchen, when she heard
the cat "yowl" in the living room.
"Tommy," she called sharply. "Stop pulling the cat's
tail!"
"I'm not pulling his tail, Mama," answered Tommy.
"I'm just standing on it. He's doing all the pulling!"
Tommy's a lot like you and me.
Something happens, and we put the blame
    on the cat,
    on the other kids,
    or even on "things."

We drop a plate on the floor while doing dishes
— and it breaks. But we don't say, "I dropped it,"
or "I broke it." We say, "It fell!"

We drive a nail over flat, and then we fuss, "That
old hammer — look what it did!"

We throw a ball through somebody's window —
and point at a friend saying, "It was *his* idea to play
here!"

We surely are good at making excuses and blaming
somebody or something else.
But God wants us to be good
    at being honest,
    at taking the blame for the things we do wrong
    and for our mistakes,
    at working to do better so our "boo-boos" will not
    happen again.

Practice saying
   "Yes, I did it."
   "I'm sorry."
   "Now that I know better, I'll try hard not to let it
   happen again!"

The Three Sons

In Russian folklore there is a story in which an old man sits at the village well listening to the splashing of the water. Three women stop with two large pails each, to fill them at the well. They are talking of their sons!

The first mother is saying,
"You should hear my boy sing.
He sings like a nightingale."

The second mother says,
"My son has such skill, he can throw a stone out of sight . . . and catch it in his hand again!"

The third mother is silent!

"What does *your* son do?" the others asked.
"He's just an average boy, like many others," was her answer.

The three women pick up their heavy water pails, and as they leave the well, their three sons come to meet them.

One sings like a nightingale.

One throws a stone so high it can't be seen, and then catches it again.

The third goes to his mother — and takes her heavy pails to carry them!

The women turn around to see the old man and call,
"See — our three sons!"

"Three sons?" says the old man. "I can see only
one!"
Do you know which one the old man had in mind
and *why*?

Birthdays

I'll bet you've had birthdays — and all the things that
go with them, like
birthday cakes,
    birthday presents,
        birthday parties, and . . .
            birthday spankings!
Sometimes you think you could have done without
the spankings, but really, birthday spankings are kind
of important! They are a way for those who love you to
let you know they are remembering every year of joy you
have brought to them by just being you!
So, if you are six years . . . or nine years old . . . your
folks, and your brothers, and sisters, and friends will
chase you, and catch you, and spank you six or nine
times — one for every year that has passed.
But, they never stop with that!
    They always give you an extra one "to grow on"!
        . . . and maybe another one "to be good on"!
It isn't only the wonderful *past* they are thinking of;
they are hoping and praying for an even better *future*!
Today, as we celebrate America's birthday,
    we give her (*correct number*) imaginary
    spankings
        in appreciation of all those past years.
But we are hoping and praying for an even better future for her, too; so we give America an extra one "to
grow on" . . . and another one "to be good on!"

[For use on the Fourth of July weekend]

What Would the Whole World Be Worth — If We Did Not Fill It With Love?

A certain traveler was going down the road to the big city when suddenly he fell into a deep and treacherous pit! He was hurt, so even though he tried hard, he couldn't climb out. There he lay, injured, hungry, and helpless.

By-and-by there came other travelers on their way to the city.

The first was unconcerned — just too busy with his own affairs and the road ahead to pay much attention. He hardly noticed, and gave only a glance.

The second was interested — he said, "Well, I've never seen anything like this before. I wonder how it happened? Do you suppose he'll ever be able to get out and go on his way again?"

The third had nothing to offer but criticism — "The crazy fool. Didn't he know better. I always did say most folks are too dumb to keep out of trouble."

The fourth exclaimed, "Hum, hum . . . glad *I'm* not in that fix. Thank God I'm luckier than that!"

But the fifth was sympathetic. "Now isn't that a shame. I *do* feel so sorry for him!"

The sixth was so touched by the man's plight that he threw him a piece of bread!

Then a Christian came along. He didn't say much, just "Hey, that's my brother!" And, what do you think he *did*? He climbed into the pit where the unfortunate man was; put his arms around him; lifted him out; and took him along with him on the journey to the big city!

What do you think God wants you to do when someone is in need and hurting?

Jesus said, "By this shall all men know that you are my disciples — if you *love* one another!"

You know a song, and I hope you sing it often, no matter where you are. It's the one that goes like this:

How beautiful is the green earth,
   The stars in the heavens above . . .
But what would the whole earth be worth —
   If we did not fill it with love, with love,
   If we did not fill it with love!

Trap — Beware!

For almost a week, a mousetrap with a big piece of cheese had been set directly in front of a certain mouse-house. Then one morning, crushed beneath its powerful grip, was found a young mouse.

I suppose when Papa Mouse first discovered that the trap was there he called a family conference. There must have been Papa Mouse, Mama Mouse, Sister Mouse, Buddy Mouse, and Squeaky Mouse (the baby). I expect Papa Mouse pointed to the trap and asked, "Do you know what this is?"

"I don't know," Squeaky probably squealed, "but there's a piece of cheese hooked to it, and I want it."

"Don't be silly," said Mama Mouse with alarm, "that cheese is a *trap*, put there just to tempt a foolish mouse like you. If you tried to get that cheese, the trap would 'snap' — and probably kill you!"

"Aw," bragged Buddy Mouse, "bet I could do it without getting caught. I'm pretty smart — and pretty fast — I could grab that cheese and get away with it before the trap would have a chance to close. I'm going to show the rest of you that I can do it!"

Then Grandpa Mouse — kind of old and grey with a short tail and a crippled foot — came out of his room and pleaded, "Please don't do it, Buddy. Listen to me, for I've had experience. I once thought I was clever and fast, and that it was the smart — and daring — thing to do. Please stay away!"

But Buddy figured Grandpa was too old-fashioned to know anything, and that the rest just didn't feel the sense of adventure that thrilled him — so, he went ahead and tried . . . and got caught!

Life for boys and girls is just as full of traps as it is for mice. And all those traps have "bait" which makes them look attractive and good. Boys and girls are tempted to take a chance because it seems like the smart thing to do, to be brave and try to get by without getting caught!

Believe it or not, sometimes parents and grandparents know what they are talking about. What they are saying is for your good — and the *really* smart thing to do is to — LISTEN!

Don't be surprised if sometime this week ... whether your name is Peter, Tommy, Jim, Diane, Pam, or Mary, somebody yells, just when you are on the verge of doing something foolish,

"All right . . . Buddy Mouse!"

Be The Best

Once there were three bakers whose shops were close to each other on the same street. Of course, each was always trying to do more business than the others — and the competition was keen.

One day, the first baker stood behind his counter trying to figure out how to get ahead of the other two. "I've got it," he cried. So, he put up a huge sign, "Best baker *in America*!" Pleased, he went to work in his shop.

But when the second baker saw that sign, he was determined not to be outdone. So, he put up a bigger sign, "Best baker *in the World*!"

Can you imagine how the third baker felt, when he read those two signs? At first he felt completely beaten . . . but then, he sat down to think about it — and pretty soon his face brightened, and a big grin showed up on it, as he painted his own ordinary size sign:

BEST BAKER ON THIS STREET!

In your efforts to succeed, don't be too concerned with being better than the other fellow; God isn't asking you to be the "best in America,"

"best in the World," or even

"best on *your* street."

He only wants you to be quite sure that you are the best *you* can possibly be!

Weeding

A little boy was busy weeding a huge strawberry patch.

Someone who stopped by to watch was amazed at the good job he was doing — and told him so,

"My, to do such a good job, you must have to know an awful lot about all kinds of weeds!"

The boy grinned, shook his head, and said,

"No, I only have to know what is a strawberry. All the rest I pull up and throw away!"

Quite a few people look at us — trying hard to live a Christian life, and to get rid of all bad and ugly things about us and inside us. Even if they don't say it, they often think,

"My, to do such a good job with your lives, you must have to know an awful lot about the bad things in the world (Evil, Wrong, Sin, etc.)."

But we can grin, shake our heads, and say:

"No — we only have to know what is Right,
                                    Good,
                                    Beautiful . . .

All the rest we pull out and throw away!"

Special Glasses

The fellow sitting next to me at the Conference meetings I attended was disturbed about something. His discomfort was noticeable; he would look at the printed paper in his hand . . . and move it closer . . . and then farther away; he would squint and strain his eyes; he would move his head at different angles to it; and then he would glance at the ceiling as if to say, "Why don't they put some stronger lights in here?" He even gave me a look which said, "Can't you do something about this?"

He couldn't see very well. Something was definitely wrong — and I knew what it was!

It wasn't poor printing on that paper;

It wasn't the light in the ceiling;

It wasn't the angle of his head;

It was his glasses — they were terribly dirty! From where I sat, I could see smears, splashes, and fingerprints. They looked as though he hadn't cleaned them for a month.

Something *was* definitely wrong — but not what he thought! It was *dirty glasses* . . . no wonder everything looked dim and hazy!

Some people look at life through dirty glasses,
    and nothing looks clean and clear;
Some folks look at life through rose colored glasses,
    and nothing appears as it really is;
Others look through "green-back" colored glasses,
    and see everything in terms of its cash value;
There are many who wear mirrors instead of lenses,
    so they see only reflections of themselves . . .
    ignoring *others*, and the *world* that needs help.

But a Christian sees life through special glasses —
    the eyes of Jesus!
        so that they see everything clearly,
            as it really is,
            in its true value,
            and beyond his own selfish circle!

Maybe things around you aren't as bad as you think — maybe there's just something wrong with your *glasses*!

The Huddle

Football is all over the TV and vacant lots these days. As you know, an important part of football is the "huddle." The players gather in a circle before each play, while the quarterback gives them the details of the next play — making sure each player understands his assignment.

But, the "huddle" is not the "game"!

The "game" is the players lining up in position, working out the play, and carrying out their assignments: kicking, passing the ball, running, blocking, tackling — all in order to get the ball across the goal line. *That's* the game!

Christians — like you and me — we also "huddle."

We gather for worship, for learning, for fellowship, *and* for "assignments": to find out what we are supposed to *do* as Christians (that's important!)

But the huddle — here in church — is not "Life"!

Life is what happens when we *leave* the church to go out and take part in the world. *How* we take our part then is what counts: how we love, forgive, help, overcome evil with good, use nice words, show pleasant faces, hand out kindness.

Now in football, a player can't even "get into the game" unless he's been in the "huddle" — you see, the "huddle" gets him ready for the game. And a Christian can't really do his best in life unless he's been in the "huddle" (church). You see, the "huddle" gets him *ready* for *life*!

Welcome to the "huddle" here!

Snap Judgment

The doorbell rang and, when the owner answered it, he found a good friend he hadn't seen for years standing there with a large, shaggy, and rather muddy dog at his side.

The owner invited them both in, but, as host, he was most displeased at the lack of common courtesy on the part of his friend — who should have left the dog outside.

The guest, on the other hand, was quite amazed at his host for inviting the dog to come in!

The two men sat in the living room and tried to talk about old times — but it wasn't easy, for the dog (after sniffing around and leaving his muddy pawprints everywhere), finally hopped up on the beautiful couch, and settled down for a nap . . .

This caused the host to go into an angry "slow burn."

The conversation was very strained — and so the visit was short. Finally, the guest rose stiffly to leave.

"Aren't you forgetting your dog?" asked the host, icily.

"My dog? That's not *my* dog," replied the guest, "I thought he was *yours*!

How often people pass judgment on each other,
        jump to conclusions,
        treat each other in an ugly way,
        hurt, and make each other unhappy — and
all because of the way things *look*, even before they know the way things *are*!

Had you noticed? Make up your mind to *be different*!

Light Of the World

A fable from India tells the story of a merchant who was getting old and ready to retire — and wanted to know which of his two sons would be the better choice as manager of his affairs after his death.

He finally devised a test, in which he gave each son a coin, saying, "Go and buy with it something that will completely fill this house." The house was large and had several rooms — and the coin was small. One could hardly imagine buying enough of anything with it to fill the house.

The elder son didn't waste any time. He went to the market place and priced all the "bulky" items like cotton and feathers — aiming to buy whatever he could get the most of for the money he had. He finally decided on straw, buying all he could and carrying it home. Disappointed, he found that although there was an awful lot of straw, it was scarcely enough to cover all the floors.

The younger son took a while to think. Whatever it was with which he would fill the house, it would have to be special. So, he went to find it. Finally, he came home carrying only a small package! His older brother laughed, "What can you possibly expect to accomplish with that, when you can see how meager all my huge bundles of straw turned out to be?"

But the younger son said nothing. Instead, he opened his little package and took out some candles. He placed *one* in each room, and when he had lighted them all — the house was *filled with light*!

Jesus told us that *we*, his followers, are to "fill the whole world" with something special! "How can we possibly do it," we worry, "we have so little to do it with?" Oh, but we forget that we have *love*, and *kindness*, and *helpfulness*, and *goodness*! It takes so little of these to fill the room where we are — and the *world* we live in together.

Do you suppose Jesus was thinking of these when he said, "You are the *light* of the world"?

A Penny

A penny is pretty small stuff. It hardly buys anything;
it's barely good for sales tax. It takes more than a hand-
ful for a little fun at a carnival, and more than you would
want to carry for new shoes. A penny is pretty small stuff
— hardly worth fooling with.

And yet, sometimes a penny gets to be

    big as a person;

    bigger than a house;

    the biggest thing in the world!

How? When I hold it too close to my eye!

    then it completely covers you —

        and I act as though you weren't there;

    then it blots out my home —

        and I act as though I didn't have one;

    then it keeps me from seeing flowers, trees,
    clouds —

        and I act as though the whole world were
        nothing but the dark side of a penny.

Isn't it foolish to let a little thing like a penny get
so "big"? Or any "trifle"?

Once a wife had a habit of stirring sugar into her
coffee in a way which annoyed her husband. He got to
holding that annoying habit so close to his eye that he
could no longer see all the loving things she did. It broke
up their marriage.

Once a buddy disagreed with his pal while they were
building a hide-out. His pal got to holding the argument
so close to his eye that he could no longer see all the
fun they'd had. It broke up their friendship.

Once a boy got interested in model airplanes. He got
to holding his hobby so close to his eye that he couldn't

see his responsibilities around the house and school. His family was really unhappy with him — and he flunked his grade.

Learn to handle pennies like pennies ought to be handled . . . pretty small stuff.

Learn to handle trifles like trifles ought to be handled . . . pretty small stuff.

Give your attention to the really "big" and important things. Jesus said, "First things first!"

Silent Whistle — Silent Speech

I've been anxious to show you this special whistle. Here, let me blow it for you. Did you hear it? Okay, I'll blow it again. No? Of course you didn't hear it — because you are not a dog! But any dog within a block of here did, if he was paying attention.

You see, this is a special whistle made for calling your dog, without bothering or disturbing the neighbors on your street. Here, I'll blow again.

You say, "Mysterious, magic! A silent whistle, yet a dog can hear it!" Well, it isn't really "silent." In fact, it has two notes, pitched very high. Your ear just isn't made for that. But a dog's ears are, and if he's paying attention, he can hear this whistle.

When you think about that, then it's not so hard to understand about prayer. How can you pray to God?

Maybe without even moving your lips,
with no sound *your* ears (or anyone else's) can hear;
just the deepest dreams of your heart . . .
and be *sure* God knows!

Mysterious, magic? No, he uses a kind of "silent speech"! Your ears aren't made for it, but your *heart* is . . . and if you are paying attention, your heart will know what God is saying . . . about right, wrong, and what you can *be* and *do*. Pay attention, and you'll "hear" his "still, small voice"!

(*Actually use a silent dog whistle.*)

Like A Hole In Your Sock

Guess where I got the idea for today's Children's Sermon? From a TV show!

Well, the father and his son-in-law were terribly angry with one another — each had done something which upset the other, and neither was about to forgive the other and "make up" — never, never, never!

Then, the mother recalls for them how *her* mother had always said that:

carrying a grudge is like
    having a hole in your sock;
if you don't *do* something
    about patching it up right away . . .
it just gets bigger and bigger
    and uglier and uglier!

We all know things about holes in our socks — and about carrying a grudge — which prove the mother was right.

Do you feel like bowing your head, with mine? Let's ask God for the forgiving spirit which "patches things up" and makes them right again . . . with *love*.

Simple Simon

Most Mother Goose rhymes and children's jingles have a lot more meaning than many people notice. Take Simple Simon, for example. (You've known that one for a long time.)

Simple Simon met a pieman going to the fair.
Said Simple Simon to the pieman, "Let me taste
    your ware."
Said the pieman to Simple Simon, "Show me first
    your penny."
Said Simple Simon to the pieman, "Indeed, I
    haven't any!"

The deal was off! No penny — no pie.
I guess we all go through a Simple Simon stage —
when we think we can have whatever we'd like (and there
are so many nice things) *without paying the price for it*.
But life demands, "First, your penny!"
You see someone wise and informed
    and say, "I'd like to be educated."
But are you ready to pay the price . . . day after
    day in school — learning and studying?

You go to a ballgame
    and say, "I'd like to be a pitcher."
But are you ready to practice every day?

You'd like to be *great* . . . but are you ready
    to forget yourself and give yourself away?

You want to *be a Christian* . . . but are you ready
    to sacrifice popularity and do difficult things?

Sooner or later, all of us have to learn that *everything worthwhile has its price* — and that we can't have whatever we'd like 'til we are willing to pay that price!

A Weight Can Be A "Lift"

I wonder if you know what these big and clumsy iron things are? Some of you do, because you've seen them hanging from the old cuckoo clock in your grandparent's house. Maybe you've even felt sorry for the cuckoo clock, having to hold up all that weight day and night — each one weighs about two and a half pounds! Perhaps you've thought, "How much easier it would be if the clock could just hang there without any weights."

But, then the clock wouldn't run . . . or tell us the time . . . and "cuckoo" cheerfully about it.

For you see, it is these weights hanging on chains that pull the wheels of the clock around. Without these weights the clock would be worthless!

Sometimes *we* complain about the weights we carry, and think life would be much nicer if we didn't have to carry any. We think:

Why do I have to go to school and study?

Why are there dishes to do every day?

Couldn't it be that the grass would grow only "so" high . . . and weeds would know enough not to grow where people want flowers?

And how about "no net" to stop the ball when you're playing volleyball?

How about no broken arms, no appendicitis, no trouble, no sadness?

But, as with the clock, these things are the weights that turn our wheels . . . put us into action . . . help us to be something useful and worthwhile!

Once I went to visit a man in the hospital — a man

who had been severely burned and almost cooked to death inside a foundry furnace. He was lying there bravely, almost completely covered with bandages, and we talked about the cuckoo clock. He was quiet a minute, and then responded,

"Yep, it's when we are carrying some heavy load, that *we are at our best*!"

Quit whining about the "weights" you carry . . . and let them turn some wheels for you!

(*Use cuckoo clock weights as illustration.*)

Fall Forward

I guess you wouldn't call me a football fan, as I know some of you are. But, I do enjoy watching the game once in a while, and no matter who is playing or what part of the game I happen to see, I always relearn an important lesson (one which every good football player must learn sooner or later).

When you are running with the ball . . .
    and are tackled . . .
        and are about to go down —
           fall forward!

Over and over again, when a player gets the ball, I see him *try* to carry it across the goal line. He usually fails to do that. He gains a few yards, and then he's knocked to the ground — stopped.

But, if he possibly can, he *falls forward* — making even his fall add to his gain.

Actually, in football, the goal line is finally crossed, not by one great successful run, but by a series of failures . . . and falling forward helps!

All of you are playing a game called "life," and you want to succeed at it. But each of you must know that things will happen to make you "fail" and "fall" many times.

You will be tackled by others, and you'll stumble over your own feet; but, if you are wise, you'll make up your mind now, that, if you have to fall — it's going to be forward!

Your failures are not going to "set you back." You are going to make even your failures "put you ahead." With God's help, when you are about to go down, you are going to *fall forward*.

Buckets

I've heard people say, "I just don't get anything out of going to Sunday church school or church. I just sit there and squirm and wiggle, or daydream, or whisper, or giggle." I've heard children *and* grownups say that!

Do you think we could figure out *one* good reason why this may be so?

Suppose it were raining right now, and I told you that I've had a bucket outside the front door of the church ever since it began to rain. Then I asked you, "Tell me, how much water is in the bucket?"

You'd answer (very wisely), "That depends:
on the size of the bucket —
and how hard it's been raining!"

Those things *would* have a lot to do with the amount of water in the bucket, wouldn't they?

Then, suppose I told you, "Here it is, Sunday morning, and Sarah is in church today. Then I asked you, "Tell me, how much is she getting out of it?"

You'd answer (very wisely), "That depends:
on the size of Sarah's brain —
and how much there is for her to get!"

Those things *would* have a lot to do with how much good Sarah gets out of church.

But haven't we forgotten something that has even more to do with how much water is out there in the bucket? Doesn't it really depend on whether the bucket is "upside down" or "right side up"!

And haven't we forgotten something that has even more to do with how much Sarah gets out of church? Doesn't that depend really on whether Sarah is "upside down" or "right side up" . . . whether she comes wanting to catch something in her bucket (*indicate head*) or not!

Whenever you come through the door for Sunday church school or church, say a little prayer, "God, help me to be 'right side up' this morning."

(*Illustrate with small bucket throughout.*)

Thread

Well, what's this? (*Actually pick up a piece of thread from the chancel rug, your robe, or whatever.*)

A piece of thread! Some ways you look at it, it's worth very little. There are many tasks for which it simply does not measure up. It's no good for
lifting a bucket out of the well,
    towing an automobile, or
        tying a package for mailing.
But, it's *just right* for
holding things together (very quietly but surely)
    like your dress or shirt, or my robe;
    The world couldn't do without thread!
Like thread, boys and girls, I'm sure *you* often feel — as all of us do sometimes — worth very little, weak, and insignificant. There are many tasks for which *we* simply do not measure up. You're no good, as President of the United States (just yet), or opera star — you couldn't even make "best ball player of the year"!

But, like thread, there are some things for which you are *just right* — as you are!
Things like: holding the family together,
        holding your friends together,
        holding us together at church,
    even holding the world together,
        all very quietly — but surely!
Try doing it — and see. The world couldn't do without thread
        or *you*!

Taming The "Wild"

What's the hardest thing in the world to "tame"?
Some would say a lion! Well, they *are* very big, and strong, and ferocious, but I saw one so tame that a man could put his head right into its mouth. At almost any circus we can see trained lions and tigers, dogs, horses, seals — even elephants (large as they are) can do amazing tricks.

I read a story about a man who had a trained fish. When the man whistled, the fish would jump out of the bowl where he lived, into the man's hand. I hardly believed that — until I saw what goes on at Sea World!

Once in New York City, I went to see a flea circus. Yes, *fleas* — dressed in tiny costumes,
                    trained to dance,
                        and push merry-go-rounds,
                    to pull chariots,
                        and race one another!

It seems to me that if people can train elephants (as large as they are) and fleas (as small as they are), they ought to be able to tame almost anything.

But, the Bible reminds us of one thing that is *almost impossible to tame or control*. Can you guess what it is? Our tongues! Truly, almost nobody can — I can't control yours, and you can't control mine! Nobody can tame or control the tongue — *except the person who owns it*.

If we really work at it — and ask God's help — we can tame our tongue:.

    not to lie, but to tell the truth,
    to say kind and helpful things, instead of mean
        and bitter things,
    to speak good thoughts, not empty, silly words.

Is your tongue still "running wild" — or have you be-
gun to tame it?

The *hardest* thing is to train our tongues to *be quiet*
... so we can listen ... keep from hurting folks by what
we say ... hear ourselves think ... and hear God speak!

Beware of your tongue — it's in a slippery place!

A Proud And Happy Feeling

Would you like to know how to get a wonderfully proud and happy feeling?

First, you have to be willing to do a helpful deed for someone.
You also have to be able to keep a secret!

To get this feeling I'm talking about, you have to do a helpful deed for someone (and I'm sure you'd have no trouble with that) . . . and then, *not tell anyone about it*. (That's the hard part!)

Usually, when you do a good deed, you feel so proud and happy about it that you want as many people as possible to know, so you make sure they find out — by telling them! How disappointing it is to discover that this takes away some of the good feelings you had about what you did!

Try, for *one* day, to help as many people around your house and neighborhood as possible . . . without anyone knowing who's doing it — and without expecting them to brag about you. By bedtime you'll probably be bursting to tell *someone*. But, don't! Try the second and the third day, and you'll begin to get that super wonderfully proud and happy feeling I was talking about, as you hear someone say,

"Well, the kitchen sink is scoured . . . I wonder who did that?"

"What do you know — the garage floor's been swept, and I thought I'd have to get at that myself!"

Or when you just see less tired and more cheerful

looks on the faces of the people you've helped. Try it
... and let me know next week how you make out. No
— that would be "telling"!

Just keep the happy secret to yourself!

Don't Point

There sure are lots of times when we have occasion, and the "right," to point a finger and say:
you're cheating,
 lying,
 selfish,
 unfair,
 hateful . . .

But when we do, it's also a good idea to remember —
 three fingers are pointing right back at *us*
  to remind us of things in *us* which are not as
  they should be!

(Demonstrate with pointing finger and obvious three remaining fingers.)

Jesus said,

"Why do you call attention to the speck in your brother's eye, and overlook the whole big stick in your own?"

Now, he didn't mean we should ignore the other person's faults; he just wanted us to be sure that, at the same time we are pointing them out, we are not forgetting our own —
so we can do something about fixing them!

Just Checking Up

A young boy stepped into the phone booth at the drugstore and made a call "Hello . . . Is this Mr. Smith? . . . Do you need a boy to run errands for you, and to take care of the store now and then?"

(But it was beginning to sound as though Mr. Smith already *had* a helper.)

"Are you sure you don't need *another* boy, if you already have one? . . . Is he able to handle the job okay . . . Thank you, Good-bye."

As the young boy left the telephone booth, a man who had overheard stepped up, patted the boy on the head, and said,

"Don't let that discourage you, boy. I'm sure — if you keep trying — you'll succeed in finding a job. Someone is sure to want a fine boy like you."

"Oh, I've got a job — I was just calling my boss to 'check up' on myself!"

Let's figure out ways of "checking up" on ourselves . . . to see whether we are measuring up to what *we* want *ourselves* to become.

Actually, that's one of the things we do here at church, isn't it!

Weaknesses

How is school? I hope you are getting along well, and that you like it.

One boy I heard about is worried. He came home and announced, "I'm in an awful fix."

"Why?"

"Teacher says I have to write plainer — so she can read what I write."

"That should be easy enough."

"Yes, but if I do, she'll find out I can't spell!"

And, that's how it is sometimes . . . if you fix up some little weakness, you seem merely to uncover or expose a bigger one.

That's why some people (including grown-ups) refuse to do anything to improve themselves.

They'd rather things stayed just as they are with them. They feel safer — as long as the big weaknesses lie hidden under some smaller ones.

But, they don't feel happier, do they?

A good place to get started at improving is with the little weaknesses. Then, we're in better shape to lick the big ones!

Being Brave

The newspaper carried the story of a fireman on a locomotive who jumped from the front of his engine to snatch an eighteen-month-old girl from death. The little girl had been sitting in the middle of the track; there was even a picture to show how he had done it!

I always wish I could do something "brave" like that . . . don't you? But it doesn't seem we have much of a chance of ever saving a baby on a railroad track.

We are very brave in our "daydreams," to be sure. We imagine a big fire . . . and picture ourselves climbing to a high window and rescuing someone. But, when there is a real fire — the firemen always get there first.

We imagine a desperate criminal "on the loose" . . . and picture ourselves capturing him single-handedly. But, actually, real criminals are hard to find — and the police usually find them first.

We imagine a tragic disaster . . . and picture ourselves trudging twenty miles to report it to the world and bring help to the victims. But, when there is trouble — someone has already phoned to tell the authorities before we even find out about it.

We may never be asked
> to rescue someone from a fire;
> to capture a criminal single-handedly;
> to trudge twenty miles with important news.

But, *one* very brave thing we *are* asked to do is
> simply to stand for what is right —
>> when others do not;
>> when others make fun of us for it;
>> when others encourage us to do wrong;
>> when we ourselves kind of *want* to do wrong!

There's a *real* chance to show how brave we can
   be — with God's help.
Be strong and of good courage,
      fear not, nor be afraid —
For the Lord, your God, it is he that will go with you;
      He will not fail you . . . nor forsake you!"

Sticks

I asked (*children's names*) to gather some sticks for our Children's Sermon this morning . . . and to get good straight ones! Here they are! What do you think of them? Not bad, are they? Thanks, (*children's names*).

Of course, some *are* better than others — and some are *worse*. Here's one. It might be hard to find one straighter than this.

Here's another . . . I believe this is still better.

Here's one; compared to these other two, it's *really* crooked.

Ah, then there's this one. Compared to all the rest, it is the straightest.

So, finally, we have them all lined up and labeled: (*Illustrate*.)

crooked,
not so crooked,
straighter,
straight.

But, look what happens when we hold them up to a stick that is *truly straight*! (*Compare to a yardstick*.)

Even the best is far from straight — they're *all crooked*!

As long as one stick is compared to another, it is always possible to find a crooked one that makes the one you have look good.

As long as it's one person compared to another, it is always possible to find someone worse than *you* are!

Sure: it isn't hard to find someone
"dumber" than you on a test,
more lazy about his work,
more "crooked" than you,
and that makes you look *pretty good*!

But, when you put yourself next to Jesus Christ for comparison, it's pretty plain how far you are from being as "straight" as you ought to be.

Now, these sticks will always be like they are — never any "straighter." They'll have to stay this way forever. But, *you don't* have to stay as you are. *You* can become "straighter," "straighter," and "straighter" . . . closer and closer to the "straightness" of Jesus.

(Of course you will want to use sticks actually gathered by some of your listeners.)

How Are Your Ears?

How are your ears? I don't mean how "big"; I mean how "good." Could you hear a pin drop? (*Drop pin on lectern*.) Then your ears are *very* good! But sometimes our ears can be very good and *still* not hear what we are meant to hear.

Sometimes when we are at the mall, a friend will call to us . . . and we go on our way unaware of it. The noise drowns out the sound of the voice we ought to hear.

Our ears are all right —
We just don't have a chance to hear!

Now and then we have the television or the boombox turned on to some mindless program, or an ad for used cars . . . when there could be good music, some important news, or an inspiring story to listen to. We are missing the sounds we ought to hear.

Our ears are all right —
We are simply "tuned in" to something else,
without any idea about what we are
missing.

In addition to these ears which we can plainly see on the outside — each of us has "inner" ears, too! I am sure that your "inner" ears are *very* good. Good enough to "hear" God's "voice" in "here." *(Indicate heart)*

If you don't hear it,
it's not because your "inner" ears are bad!
It's because:
the noise drowns Him out;
you don't want to listen; or
you're tuned in to something else.

Get away from the noise. Go apart to think and to pray.

Learn to say, "Speak, Lord. I want to listen."
Turn away from other voices. Pay attention to
God.

Medicine

Have you ever been sick enough to take medicine? Of course. Was it a pill, or something syrupy? Were you happy about it? No . . . at least not at first.

You probably yelled, kicked, squeezed your mouth shut tight, and said, "I won't!" Maybe, if you had the chance, you even hid it in a shoe or poured it into the sink.

But, gradually you got smart. You learned that medicine is there to do you some good . . . and that the only way it can is for you to take it — even if it's hard to take or has a bitter taste.

And so, now you gladly take medicine — so it can make you well!

Boys and girls, I hope you will keep on that way — willing to do what is good for you,

even when it isn't easy or pleasant!

So, as you grow up and find yourself "sick" — not so much in body, but in spirit . . . with anger, hate, jealousy, selfishness, pride, and godlessness — you won't balk and resist, or toss it away, but you'll be ready to take medicine that will make you well again.

The Bible tells us what medicines to take:

for "anger" — forgiveness and apology;
for "hate" — love and helpfulness;
for "jealousy" — contentment and concern for others;
for "pride" — simple humility;
for "forgetfulness of God" — prayer.

This medicine is sometimes "hard to take,"
    but it's *for our own good,*
        and, the only way it can possibly help us is
        for us to *take* it!

(*Illustrate with bottle of aspirin and cough medicine.*)

Tool-Box Or Trash-Can?

You probably know someone who is a carpenter. Then you know that every carpenter owns a big box with a handle on it . . . full of different things.

Whenever he is called to do a job he grabs this box . . . and off he goes.

What does he have in the box? Tools! Of course (saw, hammer, pliers, screwdriver, etc.). He can't use them all at once, but when different jobs come up, he is prepared. A wise carpenter picks a good assortment of tools, and *good* tools, too, so that he can do the best possible job.

But, what would you think of a carpenter who filled his box with woodscraps, a hammer handle, some bent nails, sawdust . . . trash . . . and then, when called to build a house, would tear out with his "trash box"?

He'd have an awful time of it! Wouldn't you hate to see the house he'd build?

Well, what kind of carpenter are *you*? We are all builders, you know — building our lives. Each of us has a "box" (*point to head*) with "two handles" (*point to ears*) which we "grab" and take with us every time we are called to do a part of the job.

What's in your box?

Good "tools" to build with — like knowledge, ideas, fine thoughts, things that help you do good work? (I'm kind of looking forward to watching you build a wonderful life!)

or

"Trash" — like a dirty joke, mean thoughts, angry talk, wisecracks? (You'll have an awful time at the job . . . and I'd hate to see the life you'll build!)

Looks

Boys and Girls, you *look good* to me!
But I wonder if *you* like your looks?
A surprising number of people *don't* like their looks.
It takes over 4,000 plastic surgeons in the U.S. to keep
up with the people who want their faces "remade" and
then, only a few people are satisfied with the way it
works out.

You see, most of them insist on blaming their troubles on their "looks"
their nose is too big, or bent;
their mouth is too crooked;
their chin is too pointed or droopy;
their wrinkles too deep and noticeable.
This has given them an "excuse" for their troubles.

Now, after their surgery, they no longer have their
excuses — but they still have their troubles — and that
makes them more unhappy than ever!

Most of us blame our difficulties and troubles on
"outward" things:
if only we had a different face;
if only we were taller . . . or shorter;
if only our teeth were straighter;
if only our ears didn't stand out;
if only we were blond . . . or brunette — things
would be different . . . better!

But, usually, the trouble is really *inside* us . . . because of what we are there.

Most of us can't change outward things (like those
in the list above). But we *can* change what we are inside! (Paul says the "inward person is renewed day by
day.")

Right here at church we learn
how to make our "inside person" as beautiful and
attractive as it was meant to be — and,
how to let God help us do it.
Keep coming . . . You'll get to *like* the way you *look*!

Spring

I'd like to tell you about a man who made a large garden. In it, he planted all kinds of seeds — in nice straight rows. Everything he planted was good: radishes, tomatoes, corn, beans, a little spinach, and some watermelons, too!

He even built a high fence around it to keep out dogs and chickens.

Then he went on a trip — figuring that with the fence for protection, he wouldn't have to worry — he'd just come back later to *pick* everything and *enjoy* it.

Well, you can't imagine how disappointed he was when he did return, because, although the fence had kept out the dogs and chickens, there was mighty little to enjoy. The whole place was choked with weeds . . . and most of the good things hadn't even had a chance to grow and produce.

That certainly wasn't the way the man had wanted it!

But, he had forgotten that fences don't keep weeds out of gardens — that the weed seeds already there *grow*, spoiling the good seeds' plants and choking them to death . . . *unless*, someone goes to the trouble of *pulling the weeds out*!

Did you know that our minds are like gardens? In them we plant all kinds of fine things to grow and bear fruit — kind thoughts, helpful ideas, loving feelings. Sometimes *we* think it is enough just to "build fences" against the evil around us — being careful to keep that out. And we forget that most of our troubles come from the evil that is right inside us (bad tempers, laziness, selfishness, greed), which will grow like weeds . . . spoiling the good, and choking it to death.

That's not the way we want it — but it's the way it will be . . . *unless*, we go to the trouble of pulling the weeds of evil out!

Let's see how big a pile of "weeds" *you* can pull this week, and how *healthy* the rows of "good things" in the garden of your mind can be by next Sunday.

Repetition

Lots of people just can't figure out why it is that their "moral fiber" (that's the "stuff" that holds them together, inside, as persons) sometimes comes apart.

It's not because they don't *care* about it . . .

It's not because they don't *mean* to keep it in good shape;

It's not that they *want* it to come apart — Oh, no! It *just simply happens*!

Well, I can tell you one cause for it — one you and I can do something about.

See this piece of paper? Entirely clean and undamaged, it is like our own character, with a certain inner fiber that holds it together.

Sometimes we figure one little evil thought, word, or deed, couldn't really hurt our character . . . anymore than one little crease could damage this paper. (*Crease paper once*.) See, I can almost straighten it out again! (*Almost!*)

Then, why not do it again . . . it's a little worse, but not *that* bad . . . and doing it is fun! So, why not keep it up? (*Keep folding and unfolding until the paper comes apart at the crease*.)

Uh-oh! It came apart! — in pieces — the fiber is gone.

And if you think I'm kidding — *this* is the map we used to plan and make our trip last summer. Pretty awful, isn't it!

And what can happen to an ordinary piece of paper, or what can happen to a fine road map . . .

just by doing, over and over, some slightly destructive act . . .

can happen to *you* and *me* — inside
. . . then the fiber is gone!

Magic Carpets

Once there were three brothers, each of whom wanted to marry a certain princess. The king (her father) had promised her hand in marriage to the brother who brought to him the thing which would please him most.

Brother number one brought the king a magic tube. Through it one could see whatever one wished — no matter how far away. Think of it: a parade in New York City; grandma — miles away; even right "through" some grown-ups sitting in front of you at a movie!

Brother number two found a magic apple. Anyone who was sick only had to smell the apple to be well again. Just imagine: you have chicken pox, smell the apple . . . and the itch is gone; you've eaten too much turkey at Thanksgiving, smell the apple . . . and the stomach ache is gone; you have a friend in bed with fever, let him smell the apple . . . and he's ready to come out and play.

But brother number three came to the king with the most wonderful thing of all — for which he won the hand of the princess. It was a magic carpet. All one had to do was to sit on the magic carpet, wish to be somewhere (*anywhere!*), and immediately be there.

Of course, that was only a story; but, wouldn't it be nice if *you* had such a "magic carpet" and simple "wishing" would let you *go* places and *do* things otherwise impossible?

Well, just a minute, I know of two "magic carpets" right here in this church (*pick up offering plates*) . . . and they're *real*!

When you place your gift in this offering plate, it is as though you stepped up and sat right down on a "magic carpet" which can take you — as quickly and as surely as you can wish:

to Africa, to preach a sermon or lead in worship;
or to Equador, to be a doctor or nurse; to India, to teach school,
or to Bangladesh, to feed the hungry and clothe the naked.

You may be asked to go to a hospital with crutches or medicine for those who need them, or sit — with friendliness and caring — right next to people lonely and despairing. You might even choose to be whisked just a few blocks from here, to help a neighbor in (*your own town*).

Remember: every Sunday as you bring your offering, you place *yourself* on one of these "magic carpets" and go on some exciting journey, to some interesting place, to *do* some good thing . . . all of which, otherwise
would simply be *impossible*!

Yardsticks

I guess you know what this is: a "yardstick," of course — just like everyone else's. That's just what I don't like about it! Thirty-six inches long. If one guy measures something and says it's nine inches, the next guy will come along with one, measure the same thing, and, sure enough, same answer — nine inches. Now I'm tired of that. I want a yardstick that will measure things the way I want them to be. So . . . I went ahead and made my own!

See? *My* yardstick is marked in inches, too . . . these gold lines have variety in the spaces between them for convenience. My yardstick is (*count out*) thirty-one inches . . . or as you can plainly see, six feet and one heel long! I can measure anything with it — the Bible here, this ledge, my hand, how tall the choir members are . . . now, *that* suits me fine. So, nobody has to come around to tell me how big something is . . . *I'll take my own measurements, thank you*!

Of course, you *know* I'm being "silly" . . . just to remind you that, even though my measuring suits *me*, it is *not* correct. Nobody (even though he may try) can use his own "made up" ideas to tell how big something is — and certainly, not how right, or good, or worthwhile something is: NOBODY.

Not even a king! An American reporter visited King Farouk's palace in Egypt after he had been overthrown. In the enormous bathroom, he noticed a scale which the king had used to weigh himself. The reporter asked permission to use the scale, and was surprised to find that it "measured" twenty-five pounds light. The king had "rigged" the scale to show his weight the way he wanted it to be . . . to suit himself . . . "lighter" than he really was.

My reason for telling you this is not to give calorie-conscious parents ideas about what to do with their scales, but to show *you* another way in which people try to make up their own standards, so that things will "measure out" the way they want them to, to suit themselves.

King Farouk might have been fooling himself, but, certainly not God. And others must have been laughing at him, or pitying him. If he really wanted to weigh less, he would have done better to change himself — instead of his scale!

When we say we are "loving," is it only by some
    measure we have "fixed" to suit ourselves?
When we say we are "unselfish," "right," "good," is it
   by some measure we have "fixed" to suit ourselves,
    or is it by the "yardstick" of God?
Actually, we are being "measured" and "weighed"
    every day by "yardsticks" and "scales" which
    belong to God — and tell the truth about us.
If we really want to be "loving"
                "unselfish"
                "right"
                "good"
  we would do better to change ourselves —
    instead of the yardstick or scales.

A Boat

Somebody took me fishing . . . but what I want to tell you about has nothing to do with the fishing; it has to do with the *boat* . . . and *me* . . . and *you*!

That boat,

which had seemed pretty *big* when we carried it from the backyard, fastened it on top of the car, and handled it at the launching dock, seemed pretty *small* out on the huge lake.

It really wouldn't take much water to sink that little boat . . . pull it right down. I bet there was enough water in that lake all around us to sink that little boat 100,000 times!

Wow! Isn't it dangerous to take a boat like this out on a lake like that? I was a little frightened.

And then, it occurred to me:

not unless you let the water get *inside* the boat.

It's only the water that gets *inside* the boat that can sink it!

Just be careful to keep the water *out* of the boat. (So we were.)

Maybe you sometimes feel like I sometimes do:
a little frightened about being out on the sea of life;
awfully small, with a terrible lot of evil all around (hate, selfishness, ugliness, filth);

It wouldn't take too much of that to pull my character right down . . . take me under;

I'll bet there's enough evil around to pull me down 100,000 times!

Wow — isn't it too dangerous to live in the middle of so much "bad"?

Not unless you let the "bad" get inside you . . . It is only the "bad" that gets *inside* that can ruin you and pull you down.

So . . . be very careful . . . and you'll be safe!

Right For The Job

Do you ever "put yourself down"
— think of yourself as a square peg in a round hole
— see yourself as a "misfit"?
I like the story of John and Pat, who were building
a house:

> Pat noticed that John was throwing away quite
> a few of the nails he was taking from his pocket.
> " Why are you throwing away so many nails?"
> she asked.
>
> "Because the heads are on the wrong end!"
> John replied.
>
> "Don't be foolish," chided Pat, "Those are for
> the other side of the house!"

Whenever you feel that "your" head may be on the
wrong end . . . and you wonder whether *you* really "fit
in" anywhere, remember that *no one* is a misfit or cast-
off in the family of God.

Maybe you *do* need to get yourself "turned around,"
but don't forget — *you* are "just right" for *some* job in
God's kingdom.

Anonymous!

I hope you liked the hymn we sang this morning — "Come Thou Almighty King" (*Sing the phrase again.*) Do you know who wrote it? It was Anonymous! Another hymn by Anonymous is "Fairest Lord Jesus." Then, there is the Christmas hymn "Away in the Manger." Well, Anonymous wrote that, too. Aren't we glad he did?

Not only did he write hymns, but poetry, too; and he did so many wonderful and important things:

Who invented the wheel? Anonymous!
Who first used fire? Anonymous!
Who first pried loose a great stone with a lever?
    organized the first government?
    built the first school?
    first worshiped God? Yes, Anonymous!

Actually, most of the things that make life interesting and worthwhile we have because of Anonymous.

Who is this Anonymous? *We do not know*! "Anonymous" means "we do not know." We do not know:

who wrote those hymns;
who invented the wheel;
who first used fire;
who did many of life's best
    things.

We do not know who Anonymous is . . . but I kind of like him, don't you? He (or maybe he was a she) was

the kind of person interested in *getting things done*
. . . never mind who gets the credit for doing them!

Someday, maybe you and I can be "Anonymous" —
someday, maybe the world will enjoy some fine thing
because of *us* — even if it doesn't know *we* were the
ones responsible for it.

Someday, maybe the world will remember us
— not by name, but by enjoying and being blessed
by some good thing we did!

From The Inside Out

At the National Convention of Barbers, they pulled a "stunt" to advertise what their services could do for a person.

They went out and got the filthiest bum they could find in the gutter —

tangled hair,
scraggly beard,
dirty fingernails,
bleary eyes, and
ragged clothes.

They gave him a shave, haircut, shampoo, manicure, bath, massage, and a new suit.

Then, they marveled at the "new man" — he really looked good!

The photographer got some shots for the newspapers. The fellow himself strutted about, pleased with himself. One hotel manager was so impressed that he offered the man a job. "Tomorrow at nine?" "I'll be there."

When he failed to show up by noon, they naturally looked for him — and found him:

lying in the same alley,
his clothes dirty and wrinkled,
his hair a tangled mess,
with the old bleary eyes.

They had changed the man's *looks* . . . but they hadn't changed the *man* a bit!

That is something barbers really can't do — only God can. And he will, when a person really wants him to!

Remember:

When you feel dirty inside, don't expect a bath to make you clean.

When you discover some ugly twist in your personality, don't expect to disguise it with a beautiful pair of slick boots.

When you realize your old way is making life unhappy, just fixing your "looks" will not "fix" *you*.

Only God can change you and make you clean, beautiful, happy — and he will . . . when you really want him to!

Processional Caterpillars

"Follow the leader" is all right for a "game," and going through all those "dumb" shenanigans can be a lot of fun . . . but "following the leader" is simply foolish and dangerous as a way of life! Still — in their thinking and doing, some people are always "following somebody else."

Makes you think of the processional caterpillars in Africa — who are found in gatherings of thirty to one-hundred, but always formed into a long line behind a leader.

They have no idea about where they are going . . . except that each is following the one ahead of him, and hopes that some caterpillar up front is the leader and knows where he's going. (Well, the leader is "out front" all right, but he doesn't always know where he is going — as we shall see!)

Would you believe me if I told you that in the jungle these processional caterpillars can often be found forming a single line and going 'round and 'round a tree . . . until the "leader" has caught up with the last one in the line — and follows *him*! And they will keep that up for days. (*You may want to have some of the youngsters — introduced as caterpillars — follow the leader around the chancel until finally the leader begins to follow that last caterpillar as though around a tree.*)

I read of an experiment in which a scientist got a bunch of them to go up a flower pot (*Youngsters still going around in a circle*) containing a plant of their favorite food . . . but they never got to it. Instead, they just followed each other around the rim of the pot — until they were exhausted and died!

It doesn't hurt to *look* around now and then (*youngsters do*) *away* from the one just in front of you (*youngsters do*) and — taking God as your leader — *go a "different" way!* (*Youngsters each "take off to their seats" a different way.*)

God's Hands

(*After singing "He's Got the Whole World In His Hands."*)

Have you ever wondered what His hands look like?

Well, in front of Christ the King Church in San Diego — right on a busy intersection — there is a statue of Jesus Christ.

He is standing there —
> rain or shine,
>> day or night — like this:

(*Demonstrate*)

There are his arms outstretched to help wherever needed . . . his arms — all the way down to . . . *no hands*!

They have not fallen off or been damaged. The statue was made that way on purpose . . . to say something important:

"He has no hands — but our hands, to do his work today."

We sing "He's Got the Whole World in His Hands," but in a very real sense, *he has left the whole world in our hands*!

Now you know a little about what God's hands look like:

> like *yours* and *mine* God's love is still expressed through our actions. If our hands don't do it — it won't get done.

Who do you think God is asking to do the "good things" which need doing? Somebody else? No . . . *me* and *you*!

(*The author refers to Christ the King Church at the corner of Thirtieth Street and Imperial Avenue, San Diego, California.*)

Does It Show?

Larry had been thinking about it for a long time. Finally, he made the decision . . . and he became a Christian.

He was very happy about that, but a week went by, and then he was miserable.

He told an older man, who was a friend, about it.
"What's the matter?" Larry questioned.

"Well, what have you been doing?" asked his friend.

"Nothing!" Larry answered, shrugging his shoulders with a quizzical look, "and nobody has even asked me, so I couldn't tell them I was a Christian!"

The older man didn't say anything for a while — he just disappeared for a few minutes, and came back with a candle. (*Produce candle.*)

"How do people know when a piece of wax is really a candle?" the man asked.

"When it's giving light!" exclaimed Larry! (*Light candle.*)

"Yes!" replied the older man. "And people will know *you* are really a *Christian* —" but before he could go on, Larry finished the sentence for him,

"When I'm doing something to show it!"

Boys and girls, can *you* figure out some ways of *showing* you are a Christian?

See if you can get someone to notice this week!

Impressions

Do you really know what happens when you pray?
Maybe it will help you to understand if you think of
what happens when you take a picture!

First, you point the camera at something worthwhile.
(It may take a little time to decide — after all, you want
it to be a nice picture to keep for the future.)
Then, you focus in on that subject, hold the camera
steady in that direction — no flitting around.
Now, inside there is sensitive film, ready to let the
thing you are pointed toward make a picture (an impression) on it. The "image" on the film will be of whatever
something "out there" you have decided on . . .
But, not until you *open the shutter* (which is like a
little window) and hold it open as long as is necessary
for that something "out there" to make a lasting impression on the sensitive film inside.

Prayer is like that!
First, you deliberately point *yourself* toward *God*. (It
may take a while to decide just where you want to focus your attention; there are so many things around you
saying, "Point to me! Point to me!")
Once you have decided which way you are to be
pointed, hold everything steady — flitting and bobbing
won't do.
Inside is your very sensitive self — your spirit —
ready to let a picture (an impression) be made on it. The
"image" on *you* will be whatever "out there" you have
decided to focus on . . .
but not until you *open the shutter* of your *mind* and
heart in prayer — and *hold it open* . . .

until something of God's image,
    spirit,
        thinking, and
            way
is stamped indelibly on your life!
You see: prayer is not so much *your* chance to make an impression on *God* — as it is *God's* chance to make an impression on *you*!

(Use camera creatively to demonstrate along the way.)

Getting Results

A can of fresh paint, all mixed and ready, sat next to a house and said,

"Watch me, I'm going to paint this house and make it beautiful!"

Immediately, the big brush lying on a cloth close by said,

"Hey, that's what you think! I'm the one who is really going to paint that house!"

Which prompted the tall, skinny ladder to speak up,

"Just see how far you two get at the job without me!"

The painter, who had come around the corner unnoticed, overheard the conversation and thought to himself

"If I took the day off . . . I wonder how much painting these three would get done!"

You understand — not the paint, nor the brush, nor the ladder could do anything without the painter. But, together — in the painter's hands — they could (and would) make a dingy house look clean and bright!

You and I, by ourselves, can't really do much to make a dingy, dirty world brighter, and cleaner, and happier. But we *can* put ourselves into God's hands . . .

and then *together* and with his help, accomplish his work every day!

Cheerful Givers

Everyone here at church is talking about a special kind of giving these Lenten days — generous, sacrificial, and *cheerful*. "God loves a *cheerful* giver."

You, like all the rest of us, are trying to decide what you will give, just how much you are able to give (cheerfully) and what would be nice to keep! Maybe this true story will help you make up your mind. It did mine, when I heard it! It was told to me by missionary M. P. Davis — a missionary to India and a very good friend.

A tourist was traveling in India, visiting our missions there. In one village, he was impressed with the attractive, yet simple, new little church. He was also surprised by it, for the people living there obviously had very little money. He pointed to a man and his wife working in a small field at the edge of the village, taking turns at pulling their heavy plow to till the soil.

"Oh," said the missionary guide, "the people here love their church so much that they give generously and sacrificially toward its building and its work. Why, that very man and woman over there working in the field gave so their church could be built; their gift would have amounted to about fifty dollars in American money."

Fifty dollars! Wouldn't that have bought an ox for pulling the plow?" asked the tourist in amazement.

"They *had* an ox for pulling their plow. They sold it so that the church could be built, and its good work be done!"

"I'd like to meet those people," said the visitor admiringly; so they crossed the plowed field to where the couple was working.

"I heard about your gift. It is wonderful!" spoke the

visitor through the interpreter-missionary, "But wasn't it a terrible sacrifice — to give up the ox, for *this*?"

The man and his wife stood straight and proud, looked at each other, then smiled happily as they answered together,

"We were glad we had the ox to sell!"

I feel just a little ashamed, don't you?

Are *we* ready to give — generously, sacrificially, and *cheerfully* of whatever we have — even though it would be nice to keep?

[For use during Lent]

Failures

I got to the house just in time to hear the boy's mother "give him the dickens," for some mistake he had made. Looking rather sheepish and ashamed, he mumbled, "Gee whiz! I'll *never* amount to anything . . . I can never do anything right."

I felt sorry for him (not so much because his mother had corrected him — that probably was necessary), but because he was beginning to feel he was a failure — that there were nothing but mistakes in his life.

Do you feel sorry for him, too? I suppose it is because *we* feel that way sometimes, and know what a miserable feeling it is. Let me tell you something that may help, if you ever feel that way again:

Some of you probably know a lot about baseball, and can rattle off a list of the "big name" players any time you're asked. But I wonder if you know about the player who struck out 1330 times . . . yes, struck out! That's more than any other player in the history of baseball.

Isn't that awful? If you've never heard of him, it's not surprising. With a record like that, you'd never *want* to be heard of. But *you have* heard of him! Want to know his name?

Babe Ruth — the *great* Babe Ruth!

You see he *also* batted 714 home runs — more than any other player before him in the history of baseball.

Don't worry so much about the times you fail or
   make a mistake,
Just work hard at making up for them
   by doing more and more things "just right."
God — and even the people around you — will
   "forgive and forget" the times you "struck out."

Heaven's Gates

Do you know that the only way to get into heaven
. . . is through the back door?
If you are looking forward to marching proudly up
to some big, pearly, front gates,
      having them swing wide open while trumpets
         sound and Saint Peter smiles a welcome —
you may be in for a big disappointment!
I'm afraid you'll find those gates securely locked —
and if Saint Peter *is* there to meet you —
      he'll tell you nobody enters heaven through
      the front gates, that those gates are only
      for keeping out those who are not worthy.
But, if you keep searching,
      you'll find an obscure, little-used path leading
      around toward the back. It is rough and
      briar-lined — but there are flowers, too. At the
      end of the path is a small, plain door, narrow and
      unpretentious, yet *no one enters heaven except
      by that door.*
If you're wondering why this is so,
      you will find the answer on a sign which hangs
      just above it:

SERVICE ENTRANCE

We shall be judged — all of us —
      not by the good God has poured *into us*
      but, by the good God has been allowed to pour
      through us.
Jesus himself declared,

      "I came not to be ministered unto — but to
      minister!" which means to *serve.*

"He that would be greatest among you — let him be *servant* to the others."

As Christians, we do our best to serve others with our lives . . . and, by so doing, believe we are even taking a big step in making our little corner of Earth a little bit more like Heaven!

Joined Together

Each of you received an envelope as you entered here to worship today. The time has come for you to open that envelope . . . take out the colored paper strip and sticker it contains . . . and hold them in your hand.

That paper strip (joined end to end by the sticker) could be made into you own little "link." You'd have something, but it wouldn't amount to much. No "link" is worth very much — unless it is *joined together* with others.

In the same way, of course, *you* can just sit there and be a "link" all by yourself. You'll amount to something in God's plan . . . but not much! No "link" is worth very much — unless it is *joined together* with others.

But, it doesn't *have* to be that way; your paper strip *can* become part of a *paper chain*.

You can become part of a *people chain* . . .

joining hands, and

hearts, and

efforts with all the others here!

God does have important things for us to do . . . together.

Why don't we decide, now, to interlock our "links" in one, wonderful, unbroken chain — each paper "link" representing one of us.

You link yours with that of the person sitting next to you, and then, have the ushers join the sections at each pew's end — so that they can bring the whole chain to the altar where it will be entwined about the cross.

Won't that be a great way to tell *God* . . .

and the *world*,

that we are ready to do God's work on earth . . .
"joined together!"

*(The envelope which contains the paper "link" and
sticker might carry a message something like this:
Today, I join together with all others around me in a
promise to be a strong link in the "chain" of Christians
through all the ages — and in my own time. I pray that
all the others can count on me as we strive together to
do God's will.)*

Topical Index

Accomplishment, Be The Best, Simple Simon, Anonymous!, Failures

Action, Does It Show?, In My Mind

Adversity, A Weight Can Be A "Lift"

Advice, Trap — Beware

Beauty, Looks

Brotherhood, What Would The Whole World Be . . .

Character, Looks, From The Inside Out

Cheerfulness, Popularity Winner

Choices, *Use* What You Have, Spend It For The Best, Weeding, Simple Simon, Tool-Box Or Trash-Can?, A Boat, Impressions

Church Community, The Huddle, Joined Together

Confidence, Weeding, Thread, A Boat, Right For The Job

Cooperation, Getting Results, Joined Together

Courage, Fall Forward, Being Brave

Excellence, Spend It For The Best, Targets, Just Checking Up

Expectations, Special Glasses

Failure, Fall Forward

Faith, Just To Be With Him, Light Of The World

Forgiving, Others, Like A Hole In Your Sock

Forgiving, Ourselves, Blame, Failures

Future, Birthdays

God's Laws, Yardsticks

God's Presence, Just To Be With Him, Just Where *Is* God?

Habits, Repetition

Helpfulness, The Three Sons

Humility, A Proud And Happy Feeling, Anonymous!, Heaven's Gates

Independence, Processional Caterpillars

Intentions, Targets, In My Mind

Jesus, Special Glasses, Sticks

Judging Others, Snap Judgment, Don't Point

Listening, Silent Whistle — Silent Voice, Trap — Beware!

Love, What Would The Whole World Be . . .

Patriotism, Birthdays

Prayer, Impressions, Table Prayers, Pretzel And A Prayer, Silent Whistle — Silent Voice

Preparation, The Huddle

Pride, A Proud And Happy Feeling

Priorities, A Penny

Readiness, Buckets, How Are Your Ears?, Impressions

Responsibility, Blame

Sacrificial Giving, Cheerful Givers

Self-Dedication, God's Hands

Self-Discipline, A Weight Can Be A "Lift," Taming The "Wild," Medicine, Spring

Self-Improvement, Mirror, In My Mind, Be The Best, Don't Point, Weaknesses, From The Inside Out

Service, What Would The Whole World Be . . ., Magic Carpets, God's Hands, Heaven's Gates

Setting An Example, Somebody Is Following You

Sowing/Reaping, Simple Simon, Tool-Box Or Trash-Can?, Spring

Steadfastness, A Pot Of Glue

Stewardship, Table Prayers, Magic Carpets, God's Hands, Cheerful Givers

Talents, *Use*, What You Have, Thread, Being Brave, Right For The Job

Truth, Special Glasses

Value of Small Things, Thread

Wisdom, Light Of The World, Weeding

Words, Taming The "Wild"

Worship, Just To Be With Him, Mirrors, The Huddle

Scriptural Index

It is hoped that these messages for children can stand alone — consistent with the *Spirit* and *Truth* set forth and confirmed in the Scripture, yet not wholly dependent on some "text" (which can often become merely a "pretext" or devised "peg" on which to hang the message). After all, a concept is not "true" simply because it can be found in the Bible! Rather,
such a concept has found its way into the Bible, where it is preserved and declared for us, because life's experiences have already confirmed it to be intrinsically "true"!

Exodus 20:19, How Are Your Ears?
Deuteronomy 4:9, Tool-Box or Trash-Can?
Deuteronomy 10:12, Yardsticks
Deuteronomy 30:19, Spend It For the Best
Deuteronomy 31:6, Being Brave
1 Samuel 3:9, Silent Whistle — Silent Speech
1 Samuel 12:24, Weeding
Ezra 9:6, Repetition
Psalm 27:11, Processional Caterpillars
Psalm 33:12, Birthdays
Psalm 39:23, Just Checking Up
Psalm 51:10, Mirrors
Psalm 73:28, Just to Be With Him
Psalm 85:8, Impressions
Psalm 133:1, Joined Together
Psalm 139:1-10, Just Where *Is* God?
Psalm 143:10, God's Hands
Proverbs 4:23, Spring

Proverbs 15:5, Trap — Beware!
Proverbs 20:11, Thread
Song of Solomon 2:15, Weakness
Isaiah 50:4, Taming the "Wild"
Jeremiah 5:21, Special Glasses
Matthew 5:16, Does It Show?
Matthew 5:47, The Three Sons
Matthew 6:4, A Proud and Happy Feeling
Matthew 6:33, A Penny
Matthew 10:31, Right for the Job
Matthew 10:42, Anonymous!
Matthew 11:30, A Weight Can Be A "Lift"
Matthew 13:23, Buckets
Matthew 13:46, Simple Simon
Matthew 18:20, The Huddle
Matthew 25:25, Use What You Have
Mark 9:35, Heaven's Gates
Luke 2:4, Cheerful Givers
Luke 6:41, Don't Point
Luke 6:45, From the Inside Out

Luke 11:1, A Pretzel and A Prayer
Luke 15:18, Blame
John 1:5, Light of the World
John 13-17, In My Mind
John 13:35, What Would the Whole World Be Worth . . .
Romans 12:10, Popularity Winner
Romans 14:13, Snap Judgment
Romans 15:4, Medicine
1 Corinthians 12:4, Getting Results
1 Corinthians 14:12, Targets
2 Corinthians 2:7, Like a Hole in Your Sock

2 Corinthians 8:30, Magic Carpets
Ephesians 4:13, Sticks
Ephesians 5:20, Table Prayer
Philippians 3:14, Be the Best
1 Thessalonians 1:3, A Pot of Glue
1 Timothy 4:12, Somebody Is Following You
2 Timothy 1:12, A Boat
1 Peter 3:3, Looks
1 John 1:9, Failures
Revelations 2:10, Fall Forward

Notes: